Amazon Echo Show:

The Ultimate User Guide to Learn What You Can Do With Echo Show (tips and tricks included)

Paul Laurence

D1410154

CONTENTS

Thank you for purchasing this book!

I hope it will be useful for you. If it is so, please, leave a positive feedback on Amazon and I will be able to create more helpful and interesting content for you.

Introduction

Do you like the Echo Show?

Chances are, if you've ever used a system like this, the answer is yes. But, what about if you've never used the Echo Show? What is it? Why is it important? What are some of the benefits of it? Are there any cool tips and tricks that you can try with this amazing device? Well, the answer is yes, and they're all included in this book.

This book will give you the lowdown on what it is, how you can set it up, and how to use the Echo show to the best it can be used. Through this, you'll be able to use the features that are on the Echo Show system, along with the standard Alexa features that you know and love. By the end of this, you'll have everything that you need to know in order to use the Echo Show to your advantage, and you'll be able to use this awesome system in order to learn some of the amazing tips and tricks that will make your home easier to navigate.

For many people, being able to use your smart home devices to your advantage, control everything from your voice alone, and many other things, can be quite useful, and the Echo show is ready to help you learn how to use it. By the end of this book, with all that you're about to learn, you too can use the Echo Show in your home, and from there, you can control all of the devices that you have.

I was a bit wary about the Echo Show at first. I didn't really know if it was right for me, and you might be wondering this as well when you're looking at this system. But, by the end of this, you'll be able to use it thoroughly, and you'll be able to use it with everything that you want to use it with, in order to bring your home to stunning new levels and to really use this system in the ways that you want to. So, what are you waiting for? It's time to get started with this awesome device.

Chapter 1 – What is the Echo Show?

Your first question might be just what in the world is the Echo Show? Well, you're about to find out. This chapter will introduce just what the Echo Show is, and why you want it if you don't have one already, and what the fuss is about if you already do have one of these nifty systems.

You've probably heard of the Amazon Echo, right? Well, this takes it another step further, in that It's a bit different. You might have Alexa already courtesy of the Echo system, which is a hands-free device without a screen. However, the show is a bit different. Instead of it having a speaker to tell you information, the show also has a touchscreen in order to showcase this information. Sure, it can tell you, but if you think about it, having the Echo Show makes it much easier, since you'll have everything right there. For example, if you're looking to get some audio information on something, it can be quite cumbersome to have Alexa say all of that. But, with the Echo Show, you'll be able to directly see the visuals on this, which in turn makes it easier. It's basically a video version of Alexa, and it definitely has made a difference.

Now, along with having the Alexa system, it also works with existing Echo devices that you're already got. So, if you've already got an Echo and think it's useless, don't despair, because it's actually still useful. You can hook up the Echo systems to Drop In on people if you like, which we will discuss later on. now, it also works with the Fire TV and other devices as well, so if you've got the Fire Stick, and you want to control the TV or movie that you're watching, simply tell Alexa through your Echo Show, and it will work. You can also get Fire TV on the screen too, so it's pretty neat. It's like your own personal little planner and television system. But not only that, you can control virtually every part of your home with this.

It's currently about seven inches, and touchscreen is what you're going for. You can see notifications that you might have, whether calls texts or whatever, play videos, show lyrics while playing music, and it definitely is a great device because it works with other systems.

You can even configure this to show live feed if you need to look in on something.

It's also got a camera in it, and it definitely is pretty neat. Currently, though, the camera is mostly used as an accessory when looking at styles, so that you can use Alexa to suggest outfits in order to help make your wardrobe stand out.

This is a new and functional device, and there are even more options to this as well. Now, it's constantly being updated too with new apps and such, but of course, they might not be available yet, so keep that in mind. Currently, it's available in two different colors.

Now if you're worried that your Alexa skills won't work with this, it does. The Echo Show has more skills as well, which we will discuss later on, and for the ones that are currently there, they get an upgrade and are customized to fit the show, so that you're not losing out on anything that you're missing.

It also has eight microphones, and it is way more than the speaker. Probably one of the only problems with the Echo system up until the Echo Show was released, is occasionally Alexa might mishear you, whether it be because of other devices and the like. The show takes that out, replacing it with an easy system to let Alexa hear you, which is pretty great so that you won't have to repeat yourself. It's a nice touch, and definitely worth the effort that you're putting in.

Finally, it does include Bluetooth, so if you want to play music that's not part of the skill system, or isn't included natively in the system, as in the case with apple music, you can directly stream it onto the Echo so without any problems.

The user interface on this is ahead of its time too, showcasing everything that you need to know in terms of information, making your life easier. You'd be surprised at just how easy it is to show everything, and how it can be available for you right then and there. The Echo Show is a device that works for you, and it is definitely a unique system that can help you live your life to the fullest.

This chapter showcase the Echo Show in its entirety. We'll go into further detail on some of the key features of the Alexa system, and how they're used with the Echo Show in order to help you get the most out of this and to make your life easier as well. The Echo Show is ready for you, so definitely consider this if you're wanting to try out the new and amazing Alexa system that's right there at your fingertips.

Chapter 2 – How to Set up Your Echo Show

So, you've got the Echo Show, you're curious about the system, but you don't know how to set it up. Well, how do you do that? Chances are, you've probably asked yourself this while looking at it. Well, you're about to find out, and we'll discuss some of the important aspects to consider when setting up the Echo Show.

Location Matters

The first thing to remember is that you need to pick out a great location for this. Ideally, set up the device in an area at least 8 or so inches from any sorts of boundaries, including walls or windows. That might seem bizarre, but that can mess with the signal, and it definitely is something to watch out for. But, that doesn't mean that there aren't places to put it.

You should consider the centralized location of where you're going to put the system. For example, if you're going to be in the kitchen a lot, using the Echo Show in the kitchen is one of the best places. It's great to use when you're trying to learn new recipes, and it is definitely one of the ideal locations.

If you plan on using it in a place that's right in the middle of everything, try the living room. Your living room will allow you to have it all right there, and you can then work with the other Echo devices if you have them in other rooms.

Finally, try the bedroom. Often, one of the best locations is the nightstand, and if you need to use the Drop In function, then it's a pretty great location for this. do consider this when you're setting it up.

Setup Steps

Simple to Set Up & Use

1. Plug in Echo Show   2. Connect to the Internet   3. Just ask for music,
                            using Echo Show   weather, news, and more

Now, it's time to set it up. First, you got to download it, whether you're getting it for Android, iOS, Fire OS, or other browsers that support this. You need to download the app on some device. If you have a tablet, make sure the Fire OS is 3 or higher, the iOS is 9 or higher, and the Android OS is 5 or higher. To find this, you just open up the app store based on whatever device that you use, type in Alexa, and it should show up. You can also go to Alexa.Amazon.com if you need to do this on a web browser.

Once downloaded, you plug this into the respective outlet that you want to put it in. Your power adaptor should be included, but if not, you should contact Amazon and get one of those. From there, you will need to first choose the language you want it to be in, connect to Wi-Fi, since that's where Alexa gets all of the information, log into the Amazon account associated with the device, and then look over and accept the terms and conditions. Often, this is pretty straightforward, but remember, the Echo Show only works with compatible Amazon accounts, so it has to be under the one that bought the system.

From there, it's time to use it. That's the fun part. To begin, you need to use a wake word to get Alexa to speak to you. You want to use either "Alexa" or if you need to change it, do go to the settings on the app, and go to the wake word to change it. Obviously, you can do so at any time, but the sooner that you do this, the better.

When you speak to Alexa, do so naturally. You want to make sure that you're not using any sorts of weird voices and such. Alexa will recognize you as you go along too, and you can even do voice training exercises in order to help get the most out of the system.

The Alexa system is pretty remarkable, and this setup is just that. You don't have to do too much to get started with it, which is probably the best part. Lots of people overthink this, and they think this device will take forever to set up, but all too often, it's quite easy, and you'd be surprised at just how much work you need to put into it. From there, it's time for the fun part, which is using Alexa to the best of your abilities, and it certainly is something that you'll be able to do easily, and without fail.

Chapter 3 – Starting Voice Calls with the Echo Show

Remember, that you can totally use Alexa to call others, which is pretty great. The Echo Show makes it easy. In fact, you can even look at it without fail, and it's quite fun to use too. If you don't want to look for your phone, here is how you can use the Echo Show to call people.

Obviously, you first need an Amazon Echo Show. You will need to make sure that it's set up, but you also need to have the app downloaded. From there, you need to make sure that your Alexa app is current. The Alexa app is essentially the call center for this, so you need to make sure you have the most recent version. One big part of this is the fact that the voice chat feature is enabled, so if you've already got the Alexa app, and it doesn't have that, then do make sure to update this. All too often though, it's automatically updated once you're back onto a secure Wi-Fi network.

But, if you've already got an Alexa app and you just downloaded it, that's the most recent, so you don't have to worry as much about it. From here, you just have to go to the messaging icon on there, follow the steps, and make sure that the number that you're using, along with your name, are correct. You will have to verify this in order to ensure that you can access your contacts list.

Now, you then want to verify your contacts. The Echo Show will use this in order to have Alexa get in touch with whomever you want to speak to. From there, it will use numbers to showcase the number that you want to reach. You want to make sure that your phone is connected to the app as well when set up. You'll need to also update your contacts as well. If someone got a new number put that in. If you want to send a message to someone, they need to have an entry in your contact list, along with a number. Now, the person that you have on the contact list needs to have this downloaded and synched up as well, because if not, then it won't work. So, make sure everyone that does decide to call you does have it connected as well.

You will from here be able to make calls. To do so, you say "Alexa, call ____ " and Alexa will then call them. They'll get a notification that you're calling them.

Now, if someone does call you, such as maybe your parent is calling to check in and they're synched, you'll notice that every Echo device will ring including the phone or tablet. Obviously, if you are near a device, you can then say "Alexa, pick up" and it will do so. You can also ask "Alexa, what are my new messages" and it will play them. You can also say "Alexa, play my messages" and you will be able to hear what the person left for you.

Now, if you don't want to take a call right now, say "Alexa, ignore the call and take a message" and it will. It's quite interesting.

Messaging with Alexa

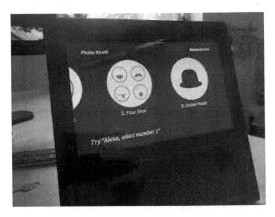

For the Echo Show, you can still tell Alexa what you want to transcribe, but it does come with a keyboard if you want to put it in yourself.

To do this, you can simply say "Alexa, message ____ " and it will then compose a message that can be sent to this person. You can then dictate what you want to say to the other person via messages. Alexa will then play it back to you so that it's verified.

If you have messages, but you're totally not able to sit down and look at them currently, you can say "Alexa, play my messages" and Alexa will then start to read back the messages including from who they belong to. That gives you hands-free messaging and is great if you're busy.

If you have a message, you will hear a chime and a yellow ring. It'll also show up when you pick up your device with Alexa installed on there as well, so you don't miss another call or message.

Now, in terms of who you can call, you can call anyone in the US, Canada, or Mexico that has either the supported Echo device or the Alexa app at hand on there. If you need to, you can voice dial a number by saying the number, if that works for you. currently though, it will only call emergency numbers if you have Echo Connect, along with a home phone line. That turns the Echo Show into more of a speakerphone, so it might not be for you. But, it gives you a more extensive range of numbers to call, including 911 and other numbers not supported with Alexa.

You can message and call other Echo systems as well. Say you got an Echo Show, but your parent has an Echo dot. They're all supported. For those that don't have one, they need to download the Alexa app in order to enable this, but that's not hard.

If you're wondering what number they see, it'll be the number that is registered on the Alexa app. Of course, if you want to opt out of it, do so by going to the Alexa app and changing that, but it's important to note that if you do so, it'll show "unknown" as your number, and it might not be something that people will answer. That's something to keep in mind.

When it comes to Alexa, it's important to understand just what you're doing with it. You can call anyone virtually with this, so long as they have an app. Drop the landlines if you want to, for this is the future. It's making it archaic, and in a sense, it's one of the best systems out there. Do try it if you need a landline but don't want to pay for one.

Chapter 4 – The Best Alexa Skills for the Echo Show

Now knowing what the Echo Show can do is quite important. This chapter will discuss some of the best skills to consider if you do have an Echo Show since it makes use of the screen and the potential that this has to offer.

Fandango

Fandango is awesome on the Echo Show, in that you can look at movie trailers without needing to put in other skills, but it also gives you a visual when you're looking to buy a ticket. If you see a movie you want to see, literally just enable Fandango, look at the movie trailers, and buy it there. You need to have a Fandango account so that you can buy these tickets easily. Since you have that all there, you won't mess up details as well.

OpenTable

This is similar to Fandango because you can reserve dinner places easily with this. It's a reservation service that while you can use it with the other Echo systems, it's not the same. However, with the Echo Show, you can see restaurants and distances in the area, and you can look at the menus as well. You can simply pick a place, choose the time, and from there confirm all of that.

Allrecipes

Allrecipes is probably the largest database of online recipes, and for the Echo Show, this is a super important app to consider. That is because, it's all there for you. If you want to look at a recipe, it's listed there, and you can cook it without having to ask Alexa to repeat it.

If you do a lot of cooking and are sick of having to ask Alexa to repeat itself tons of times, download this to the Echo Show, for it will give you visuals on the recipes, and you can use that to create amazing dishes that everyone will love.

Food Network

This is in the same vein as Allrecipes, but it takes it a step further. This is probably the ideal in kitchen visuals, since it takes the Echo Show's ability to showcase a recipe and will do so on the screen itself.

You can look at photos and the ingredients that are listed, but it also will give you actual videos of the recipe that you're creating, so you can get an idea of what you're making. This will allow you to pinpoint if you screwed something up, rectify it, and from there, create more delicious content. This is probably the future of cooking, and it does work wonders.

CNN Flash Briefing

If you want to have a quick look at what's going on in the world, get the CNN flash briefings skill. While this is available on the other Echo devices, it's better to have this all in front of you, allowing you to see everything. You can enable this and add this to your skillset, and in turn, you'll get little bits of information in the world of politics, entertainment, sports, and so much more. This is great to watch before you go to work first thing in the morning, or when you're cooking dinner, for it's all right there for you.

Nest

Nest is a great thermostat skill that can allow you to change the temperature of where you live. This is even more useful with the Echo Show, because you can take live feed of the area where the thermostat is. It also can be used for suspicious noises as well, which is pretty great, so it's basically your own at home security system that works for you.

Ring

If you don't want to get up and answer the door, but want to see who it is, you can simply use the Ring skill. This is available with the Echo Show as well, and you can from there look at a live feed of whatever is there when the doorbell rings, which is what makes it even cooler and better for you too. That way, you'll have a good idea of what's going on, and the ability to answer accordingly as needed if you must.

Uber

Finally, we have Uber, probably one of the best services to come out as of late. If you already have this on your phone, it also will show up on the Alexa skill sets too. You can get a car to come pick you up without needing to drag out your phone, so if you need a ride somewhere, Uber is right there to help you. It's also got some amazing graphics and functions really well.

With the Echo Show, it takes this a step further, allowing you to actually see the car choices, the prices, and you'll be able to get a deeper look at what you're getting before you request it, which allows you to critically look at the details of your trip in a much fitting manner. It's a great skill, and perfect for those that use Uber a lot.

These are some of the best skillsets that you can look into with the Alexa system, and they work great and are helpful for anyone looking to better their device.

Chapter 5 – Alex and Baby care (New Features to Help Parents)

If you're a new parent, you might wonder how the Echo Show can help with this. Well, you're about to find out, for here are some of the best Alexa skills to help expecting parents and parents that have already had a child take care of it in an even better manner.

Drop-In

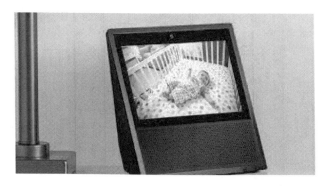

Drop-in can be used as a baby monitor. That's actually one of the best ways to check on your baby. By simply asking Alexa to do this, it will give you live feed from another Echo system, which you can put in the child's room. This will allow you to check on them, and saves money on baby monitors.

Now, it's important that for this to work, you need another Echo device, so get an Echo dot for this. It's also good to use with older kids as well to make sure that they're doing okay.

Hatch Baby

This is a smart nursery app, here prints can ask the doctor various recommended information, such as various diaper changes, how many they need, the weight of the child, when it was fed, and also how much sleep it got. You can ask Alexa how many dirty diapers the child has had, how long the child has slept, and also can record the diaper changes as well.

Now, you can use this on its own, but if you have a smart changing pad, or a hatch baby grow system, you'll be able to track this even more, including weight, and feeding amounts. The changing bed has a connected scale, which you can get insight on the development of the baby, and get doctor information in order to ensure that the child is taken care of.

Baby Stats

This will let you track the diapers both wet and stool, weight, feedings, when you've pumped, and also the baby's sleep. You don't have to track everything, just what you want to track. You simply ask "Alexa, ask the baby to add (stat you want to add) and from there it'll be added. It's best to have this along with the mobile app to track all of this correctly. You can ask Alexa to get the baby's stats as well, in order to make sure proper growth and wellness is maintained.

It's a newer Alexa skill, but if you want to check to make sure that you're feeding the kid enough, and doing enough for them, this is the way to go.

What to Expect

This is perfect for expectant mothers. To use this, you need to enable the skill, put in your information about your pregnancy, and from there, get tracking's immediately on whatever is going on in order to have a pregnancy that is both happy and healthy. If you need to, you can also adjust these dates as well, especially if you find out that your child is coming earlier. You also can use this after the baby is born too, up to the first year in order to make sure that the child is in optimal health. This is a great one to just track everything, and for those that want to make sure their fertility is in check, this can be a great skill to help, and one that can get you started on a great path. It's free too.

BabyCenter

BabyCenter also has the same sort of skill similar to What to Expect. This one as well will give you stats on the baby, what you should do next as a parent, and the like. It's important to consider using this one as well, because it is one of the first skills in this category, and it helped to pioneer the way to making sure that you get the most out of your child's health. It is good for both expecting parents to watch their pregnancy, and also for babies as soon as they are born to make sure that they're healthy.

It can be hard for expecting parents to get the job done. It's not easy to raise a child, but with the Echo Show and Alexa, you can have the visual system that you need, along with Alexa there to record information and tell you this. By using this, it can help you track the pregnancy more and more, which in turn will make it more worthwhile for everyone, and it will allow you to have a happy and healthy baby right there, with the help of the Alexa system.

Chapter 6 – Controlling Smart home devices with Alexa

Alexa Smart Home
explore compatible devices
and connected solutions

Alexa and the Echo Show can control smart home devices. How does it do it through? Well, you're about to find out.

To begin, you first need an Echo Show that is connected with the Alexa app. If you don't have that already, get one, download the app, and sync these together. Also, keep in mind the place where you've put your Echo Show. It might not seem like much, but one thing that you need to consider is that it will be controlling all of the smart home devices, so make sure that it's in an area with a strong Wi-Fi signal, and if it's not, you should definitely consider moving this. If your house is too big for Alexa to register some smart home devices, pick up another Echo dot for some extra help.

From here, it's time to set up the smart home devices. You need to get some first, and for the setup of this, you typically do it just like normal. You're going to give this a name though, so make sure that you give it something that you're okay with calling it, and something that is clear, concise, and able to be understood easily. Things such as "kitchen light" or "living room lamp" work great.

Once this is done, you need to introduce Alexa to them and get it to recognize them as well. Typically, you can say "Alexa, discover new devices" and after a few seconds, it'll scan the area and add gadgets that are found, and you'll be able to control them after.

If you don't have the ability to do so, you'll have to manually set it up yourself. You'll need to go to the smart home section, go to "smart home skills" and from this point forward you should search for the skills that you want to enable. Nest and Lutron for example require you to do this, and you need to login in order for Alexa to take control of this. You need to authorize this since it does involve cameras and such.

Next, you need to group everything. If you're wanting Alexa to control more than one similar device, you should group these together. There are also other groups called scenes.

Groups are what they literally are, which are devices that are behind one single name, such as the kitchen lights working together. Instead of asking Alexa to turn on one by one, you can group these together. To make this, you go to the Alexa app, click on the smart home section, go to Groups, and then

Create Group. Give it a specific name for it to be recognized with and then choose the devices you want to include.

Scenes are when you put some multiple devices in to certain settings. You don't create them with the Alexa app though, and instead you import scenes from the direct devices, and you can create an IFTT recipe in certain cases as well to make this.

For example, if at night you want the bulbs to be a certain brightness setting, you can make a scene with these lights and such. When you look to discover this, it'll find the scene, and you can ask for it to be activated. It's that simple.

All About IFTT

IFTTT is a specialized way to connect the hardware and services. Now, if you want to automatically have something happen when a condition is met, such as the front porch lights come on when it's dark out, you can create an IFTT recipe to help make this possible. You need to download the IFTT app and create a login for this before you begin. You can then create recipes, choose the devices that are connected to it, and then automatically generate a new recipe that can be used to help with improving your smart home.

It's still a newer system, and it's getting the kinks still fixed in them, but it's definitely something that you should consider. It will bring the dream of having a smart home that is futuristic and new to the forefront, and it definitely does help if you want to control your smart home devices all at once. Plus, this can be used not just for smart home devices, but also for personal elements of your life, such as if you miss a message, Alexa automatically notifies you on ToDo List or something like that.

With Alexa, you can control your smart home with just your voice. It's bringing homes and other devices to the future, and for those of us that want to make a huge difference in the life of our smart home, this is the way to do it, for it can totally change the way you control things, and your life as well.

Chapter 7 – How to Get Alexa to Play Music, movies, and videos

Alexa has the ability to play music, movies and videos with this amazing system. With the Echo Show, it changes this as well. Here is how you can reap the benefits of this, and get Alexa to do all of this for you easily.

Music

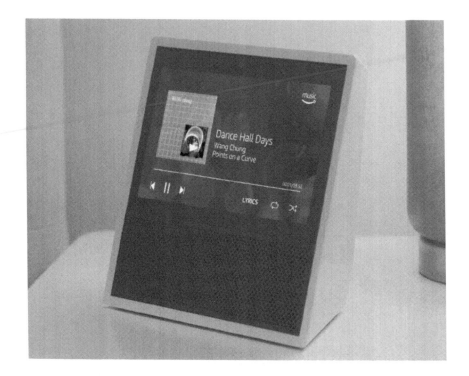

When it comes to music, Alexa has you covered. Not only that, you can now look at the lyrics on various songs if you want to see them through the Echo Show. But how do you play music? Well, here is how.

If you have a personal playlist from either iTunes, Google Play, or other various means, you go to "My Music" on the Amazon site via the computer. Put the music there, and once it's all up there, you can ask Alexa to play this by saying the name of the song, and it'll play it. You can do up to 250 songs with My Music, and that's free. But if you want to upload more, you need to get an Amazon music Storage subscription, and from there, you can play any music that you want. However, if you buy something from the digital music store or autorip eligible CDs/records don't actually count towards the limit, so keep that in mind.

You can also play it on Bluetooth. To do this, you need to make sure that you have a Bluetooth connection, and from there, you can simply choose the song, or have Alexa do so. You need to make sure these are synched up though.

To play this on multiple Echo devices, such as maybe through the house, you can go to the smart home tab, then choose groups, create group, multi room music, and from there, you can then choose the Echo devices for this, and you can custom name this too. Once you've decided it, you can create groups and that'll make those Echo devices a group. Once you do that, you can have Alexa turn these on, and then have Alexa play music, and you can control the volume of this by saying "set volume for group to level X" and it'll automatically do that. You can't do Bluetooth connected speakers currently however, so keep that in mind.

How to Play Movies on the Echo Show

The Echo Show can play movies if you so desire. If you want to watch something, you first need to enable the skills that are available that allow you to watch something, such as

HBO, Showtime, and Starz. With all of these, you will need a subscription, so make sure that you have that.

Now, to watch this, you simply ask Amazon to show you the titles based on the title itself, the genre, the actors, or other factors. You can then say, "Alexa play ____" and it will do that. You can use your voice to control the playback as well.

If you for example have a Netflix account and you want to watch the next episode of "Orange is the New Black" you simply tell Alexa "Play Orange is the New Black, Season 1 Episode 2" and it'll do that.

For Amazon video, you get this automatically with a prime subscription, and you need to make sure that your Echo Show is linked to wherever your Fire TV or other device is. You can also watch this on the Echo Show by saying "on Echo Show" if you don't have one, or if you don't want to watch it on the Fire TV. You can simply go through the library, ask Alexa "show me my video library" if you don't know what to watch, find specific titles that work for you, and look at various media based on certain actors. With all of this, you have control, and Alexa can help you out.

Watching Videos

You can watch YouTube right from the comfort of your Echo Show? How do you do that? Well, here is how.

First, you need to make sure that YouTube is enabled on this. Obviously go to the app, choose the skill, and enable it. simple as that. From there, you can say "Alexa play YouTube music" and you can from there have Alexa play various videos. You can ask for Alexa to give you video suggestions too, especially if you want to watch a video about cats, dogs, whatever it is that you want. You will then immediately be able to play what you want to watch. The cool part is, you don't even have to touch the system. Alexa will play it for you. You can then listen and enjoy whatever it is that you want to on the Echo Show.

The Echo Show is a great device for those that love to play media. You can even connect this to the Fire TV if you want to stream it, but make sure that if you do this specify whether you want it to be on the Echo Show or Fire TV, because that is definitely something to consider.

Amazon and the Echo Show are working together to give you media that you can control with your voice. It's amazing all that you can do with it, and almost magical if you think about it. You have the control directly at your disposal, and it's something that you can take full advantage of and learn for yourself, in order to get the most out of this smart device.

Chapter 8 – Alexa and Cooking

Do you know how useful Alexa is with cooking? Well, you're about to find out. We touched a little bit on this with the Allrecipes and the Food Network system, but, we're going to go into more details on how Alexa can help in the kitchen, in order to make you a killer chef that can make anything you want.

Best Recipes

Now, let's say that you want to cook something, but you're limited on ingredients, and the last thing you want to do is go to the store. Best Recipes is by Hellman's and it allows you to take ingredients that you have in order to create recipes that are totally possible. This works with both lunch, dinner, and even breakfast recipes. Now, it will email the skills, but you can ask for visuals as well if desired.

Substituting Ingredients

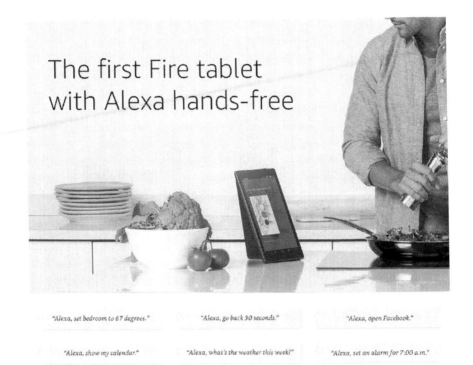

The first Fire tablet
with Alexa hands-free

"Alexa, set bedroom to 67 degrees."   "Alexa, go back 30 seconds."   "Alexa, open Facebook."

"Alexa, show my calendar."   "Alexa, what's the weather this week?"   "Alexa, set an alarm for 7:00 a.m."

Do you want to change a recipe because the ingredients aren't per your diet? Or maybe you want to cook something, but you don't have the ingredient on hand? Well, you don't have to worry about that problem, because Ingredient Sub is an Alexa cooking skill that will allow you to substitute items. It has a lot of basics on there, so it might not be fitting for complex diets, but if you're looking for healthy alternatives, this is certainly the place to go.

Cooking food Safely

The last thing anyone wants to have is to either serve overcooked or undercooked food. It's either embarrassing, or generally unhealthy. However, by downloading the Cook reference skill, it will tell you the safest temperature to cook everything, which will save you a Google search. It has most of the common meats on there, so you don't have to go too far in order to find this information, and it does work wonders for you.

Grocery Shopping Made Easy

> *"Alexa, order a picnic basket."*

Now, if you want to add items to the grocery list, but you don't feel like jotting it down constantly with a pad and a pen, you can use the Chefling skill in order to keep track of what you need to buy. But that's not all, it will allow you to know when food is about to expire, and by simply opening up the app, Alexa will do the rest of the work. You can add various items to the list, share shopping lists with others, and also check and verify expiration dates to keep your kitchen the best it can be.

Grilling King

If you've wanted to grill, but you've struggled with it, there is a skill called Grilling Time and Heat Master, which will allow you exactly how long you need to grill something, based on the meat, veggie, or fish that you're throwing on there. It'll also tell you what temperature is best, whether it should be done directly or indirectly, and even how long you should keep it there. If you've ever wanted to get good at grilling, this is the way to go, and it's so simple that practically anyone can do it themselves.

Storing Fruits and Veggies Right

The one thing that stinks is when you buy some fresh fruit or produce, and then you need up not using it, causing it to expire. You might end up putting it somewhere, forgetting about it, and then it's too late to use it. The Fruit Stand skill will tell you the best place to store a fruit or veggie, and where it should go to live the longest. Of course, it can also tell you the average shelf life too, so that you can throw it somewhere so that you don't forget it.

Spice Master

Herbspice is a skill that will allow you to become the master of herbs and spices that you should be. To be honest, lots of people don't know how to use herbs and spices effectively, and a lot don't even know of some that exist. But, this skill will allow you to get random facts about the roots, plants, and the seeds, which in turn will make you a better cook. You can even use this in herbal medicine, such as in the case of you're feeling nauseous. You can then take some ginger and it's a naturally way to stay healthy. You can also learn how to use these herbs in the kitchen for best results too.

Get Seasonal Foods

Finally, you can find out what's in season, which in turn will allow you to get various fruits and veggies into your diet in order to be healthier. You can get the Farmer's Market skill, and this will tell you what's in season around you, and you can from there go to your local farmer's market and pick up what they have to offer. Eating local and home grown will allow you to get the full benefits of these natural foods, and this skill will in turn allow you to do just that as well.

When it comes to cooking, Alexa can help you a lot, and with the skills and various helpful tidbits listed here, you can use Alexa to your advantage in order to have the best cooking skills that you can have. Gone are the days where you're fumbling in the kitchen for a recipe, for Alexa and the Echo Show can work in tandem to give you everything that you need to be the best chef you can be.

☐

Chapter 9 —The Drop In Function and How to Use It

The Drop In function is something that is useful to many, but often gets criticized back of the lack of privacy that this gives to people. But, if you bought an Echo Show, it's important to realize that you have this system, and it's a valuable function that can certainly help you. so, what in the world is it? Why does it matter? Well, you're about to find out, and you'll learn why some people love, yet also dislike this interesting system.

What is it?

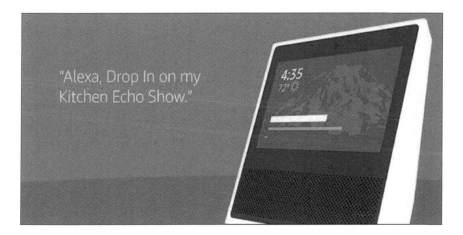

Have you ever seen those intercom systems that others have had installed in their homes, where they will press a button to check in on someone? That's essentially what this is. Drop In is a means to let users listen to the speakers on a device from one Echo Show to another, or from the smartphone app. It allows one to check in on others, or to call someone if they need to get clarification on something.

Think about it. This could be useful for those that are cooking dinner and want to let their kids know. It's a means to call others, and let them know about the state of something. It's an interesting functionality that does allow one to instantly connect to other Echo devices without using your hands, and it will allow you to check on other Echo devices not in the home as well. Obviously, it's best that you do realize the privacy nature of this, so you need to make sure that you grant permission to this, so make sure that you're okay with this. You will have to enable it yourself, so you won't accidentally do it, which is pretty neat.

How to use It

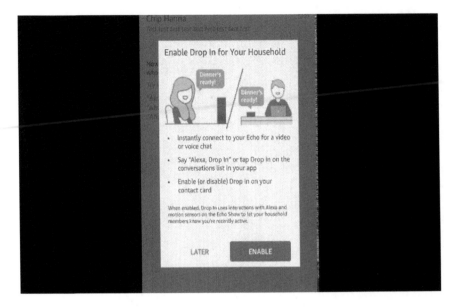

How you use it is simple. First, you need an Echo system to Drop In on, and one to start the drop in. For starting the drop in, you can use the Alexa app as well. You need to make sure that you sign up for Alexa calling and messaging, which will allow it to call and message others. It will then allow you to enable Drop In on who you want to Drop In on, such as maybe an Echo device in the playroom or something. You can then have a contact use Drop In on you if you so desire, but that is optional.

You can then say "Alexa, Drop In on ____" whether it be the name of the Echo device or the name of a contact, and Alexa will allow you to speak to the other Echo. When you do get a Drop In on the device that you have, you'll see a green and pulsing light, and you can then connect and heat everything within range. If you're using the Echo Show and so is the other, you will then be given an option to video chat. You can turn that off though if you don't want to, either by selecting it, or saying "video off" and it won't chat with you. You can also put in Do Not Disturb to block any drops on a specific device for a temporary amount of time, so keep that in mind.

If you want to have a great intercom system though that works wonders and can help, this is the way to do it. It's the future, and you can use this in a variety of ways. Try it out, see if you like it, and try to use Alexa to Drop In on others. It's a bit of a different system, but it can bring everything to the future for yourself, and it definitely is worth it. □

Chapter 10 — Troubleshooting with the Echo Show

Sometimes the Echo Show doesn't work in the way you

expect it to. This can be frustrating, and quite annoying. But, if you're worried about this not working, don't be scared. Here are some of the common problems with the Echo Show, and what to do about it.

Your Echo Won't Turn On

Sometimes, your Echo Show might just be completely unresponsive, and won't power on. This happens during the initial startup, and here are the reasons why.

Your power adaptor might be faulty. Make sure it's plugged into an outlet that works, and if there is still no power, then it's the adaptor's fault. Contact Amazon in order to get a replacement.

The other problem is a faulty motherboard. It's simple to look at the components, and if you realize that it's a problem with the parts, it's often the motherboard. This will need to be replaced, so contact Amazon.

The Screen is Frozen

Sometimes your screen doesn't respond to what you put in. There are three causes for this.

The first, is that it needs to be cleaned. This system uses LED lights, and if there are particles blocking, this can cause the screen to freeze up. Use a cloth and a screen cleaner and make sure nothing is blocking it.

Another problem is that it just might need a restart. When in doubt, you should always restart. You should unplug, let it sit for 30 seconds, and then reboot.

Finally, it might be that the circuit board is messed up. If your finger breaks the grid, it will register as a touch, even when not touching it. It might be the circuit board, which can be replaced. Contact Amazon if that's the problem.

Your buttons don't work

If the buttons don't work, and you've already tried a hard reset, it could mean that the buttons are at fault here. There are two ways to fix this, and one of them is to either clean the buttons, or contact Amazon to replace them.

You can't connect to Wi-Fi

If you're unable to connect to Wi-Fi, there are a few reasons behind this. Obviously, if you haven't reset it yet, do so, but if it's still not connecting, there are a few things that might be the culprit.

First, is that the Wi-Fi isn't enabled on the device. Put the Echo Show out of snooze mood and connect.

If that's not the problem and you've already tried other things then you've got router issues, or modem issues. It might be the culprit, and if that's the case, first turn off both of these, starting with the Echo Show first and then the router or modem. After that, turn the router back on, and wait for it to connect. Then try to connect the Echo show. If you're still getting problems, contact your ISP to see if they can have someone come out there to help you.

Your screen either has dead pixels of Lines

This is more of a rare circumstance, but if you've got dead pixels on the screen, or maybe there are lines, there are two causes for this. Of course, you could hard reset all of this, and if that doesn't fix it, it's time to check these two culprits.

The first, is that your screen might be faulty. Ultimately, this is something that would happen right away, and not something that could happen for a long period of time. Contact Amazon and see if you can get this replaced.

Then there is device interference. This is a common problem with both Wi-Fi connection, and also the screen state. If your Echo Show is neat other electronics, it might be affected by this, because of all of the signals coming out of this. Move it away, reboot it, and then try again. See if that can help you.

With the Echo Show, the problems are very minimal, but if you do realize that you're having troubleshooting issues, try these various things, and if you're still struggling, it might be best to send this to Amazon so that you can get whatever you need replaced, and to get the assistance that you need.

Chapter 11 — Useful Tips and Tricks

Now that you know about the Echo Show, it's time to take a bit of time to customize this for you. Here are a few things to allow you to get the most out of this device.

Customize your Drop In Function

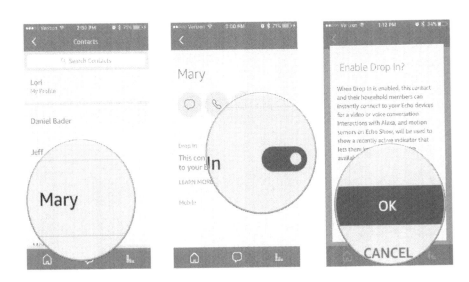

If you haven't already, customize who drops in on you. If you don't want people dropping in and trying to start audio or video calls, you can customize this by going to the Alexa app, going to the Echo Show device, choosing to drop in, and press "only in my household" which will prevent outside people from dropping in. When you turn it back on, you will need to approve which ones can drop in, so go to the Conversations part of the app, choose the contact, and then press "Contact can Drop In Anytime" to enable this.

Setting Up Do Not Disturb

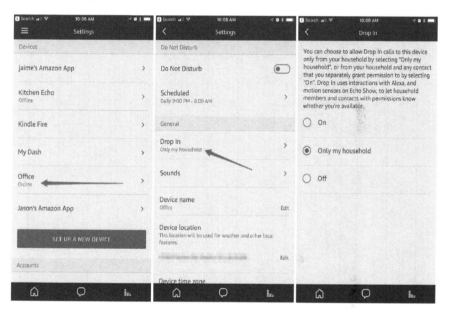

If you're overwhelmed by people messaging you or contacting you, you can enable Do Not Disturb. You first swipe down the screen at the top of the app. You should look for the on-demand button that you see to turn on the DND function, and from there, you won't receive anything, whether it be calls, messages, or other notifications. You can schedule it as well.

From the Echo Show's menu, go to Settings, move down to

Do Not Disturb and select that to set up a schedule.

Creating a Background Photo

If you're someone that doesn't like the standard background, you can upload a photo to the background from the app itself.

To do this, go to settings move down, and press the button that is in blue called Choose a Photo and from there you can choose a photo, crop it as needed, and then put it up. You'll immediately see this directly on the Echo Show, which is Neat

Adjusting the Sound

If you're a bit annoyed by the sounds that you hear, there are a few ways to adjust this. You should, from the Echo Show itself, choose the settings tab and go down to sounds. You can choose the alarm, notification, and also any sounds that you need, such as reminders. You can also turn it off if you don't want to hear any period, which is nice.

Talking Rather than Touching

If you're a bit weirded out by talking to the device, don't sweat it. However, if you want to make your life easier, you should make sure that you do try to work on using your voice for it. You don't have to, but it's nice.

You can also give Alexa commands, and if you want to opt in for touch, you can as well.

There are two ways to open up virtually anything on the Echo Show. They're either touching, or talking. You can choose either or. Talking is often a bit easier for some people, but if it still weirds you out to talk to the device, or maybe you're getting used to using it, try maybe touching the device rather than talking.

Say Cheese!

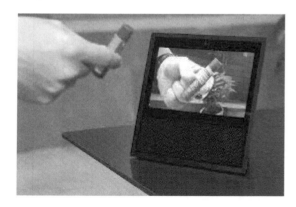

Another great function of the Echo Show is that you can take pictures with it, which is totally different from the other Echo devices. To do this, you can open up the camera app or tell Alexa "Alexa, open the camera" and it will then give you three camera options for you to try out. You can choose one, tell Alexa the number that you want, and Alexa will take a picture. You don't even have to use your fingers, you can actually have Alexa do it all for you. It's a way to totally automate all of this, and it can change the way pictures are taken.

Going home

If you're sick of having to scroll through menu after menu to go back to the home screen, fear not. Alexa can take you directly back to the home menu, and it doesn't take all that much work. Obviously, you can swipe the screen from the top of the display and press the home button, but wouldn't you like this to be easier? If you say, "Alexa go home" you'll get Alexa to take you back to the home screen, which is also kind of humorous as well.

A Digital Photo Frame

Building on what you could do before, you can actually turn the Echo Show into a photo frame. If you want to take a photo that you took with someone you love as the Echo Show background, or even have the Echo Show showcase this picture, what you do is go to Prime Photos, and from there select the album that you want to put on there. That's right, just upload the picture of pictures to there, and then ask Alexa to show this off. Simply say "Alexa, show my _____album" and the blank is whatever you named it. You can make this a slideshow, or even a singular show, whatever it is that you desire.

The Echo Show is a newer device, but that doesn't mean it doesn't already have its own unique tips and tricks. This chapter gave you the information that you need in order to get the most out of your Echo Show. Start to use this today, and work on getting the most out of this. Your Echo Show is a valuable device, and you'll realize, as you continue to play around with it, that there are so many options and functions you have yet to discover.

☐

Conclusion

As you've learned here, the Echo Show is an amazing system, and you'll learn from this as well that it is one of the vest devices on the market today. There is so much that you can do with the Echo Show, that when you begin to use it, you might not even learn everything until after a few uses. Which is totally fine. The beauty of this device, is that it's constantly being updated, meaning that you'll be getting new and innovative features each time you use it. It does its own updates too, which means that you will be getting the most recent version of every time that you use it.

Really, your next step is to start looking into getting the most out of your Echo Show. Start to play around with it. use it a little bit. Learn the system, and you will from here be able to truly utilize this great and amazing system. You won't want to stop using it once you begin, and with this book, you have everything that you need to know to totally take full advantage of it, so it's in your best interest to learn more about it as you go along.

Thanks for buying the book!

I hope you liked reading my book. Please leave a positive review on Amazon, if you want me to create more books.

I think next books will also be interesting for you:

Machine Learning

Raspberry Pi 3

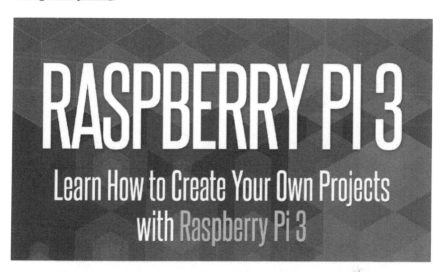

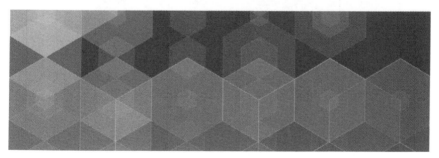

Amazon Echo

79156319R00040

Made in the USA
Lexington, KY
17 January 2018